# FUN WITH OCEANS & SEAS

# FUN WITH
# Oceans
# & Seas

## A Big Activity Book for Kids about Our Wonderful Waters

### EMILY GREENHALGH

### ILLUSTRATED BY CANDELA FERRÁNDEZ

Z KIDS • NEW YORK

Zeitgeist™ is a trademark of Penguin Random House LLC

ISBN: 978-0-593-43570-0

Map © by zeber/Shutterstock.com and Ivsanmas/Shutterstock.com

Illustrations by Candela Ferrández

Book design by Aimee Fleck

Illustrator photograph © by Artur Laperla

Manufactured in Hong Kong

1st Printing

TO NATALIE, GABBY, AND
EVERYONE WHO HAS EVER
LOOKED OUT AT THE OCEAN
AND WONDERED WHAT LURKED
UNDER THE SURFACE

# Contents

# Welcome to Our World of Water!

We call our home Planet Earth, but it should really be called Planet Ocean! Did you know that more than 70 percent of the surface of our planet is covered by the ocean? That's lots of salt water—and lots of awesome things lurking beneath the surface waiting to be discovered. For thousands of years, brave explorers sailed, swam, and even dove into the world's oceans and seas to learn their secrets. With this book, you can too!

You have probably heard the names of some of the oceans. Maybe you've even visited one. But did you know that the five oceans—Arctic, Atlantic, Indian, Pacific, and Southern—are all connected into one big global ocean? You can make it all the way around the world without ever touching land.

People used to explore our big blue world in tiny, rowed boats. Now ships the size of buildings carry goods all around the globe every day. With the help of submarines, scientists can even explore what's under the surface.

We have special names for the parts of the ocean that meet the land. Seas are smaller than oceans and are partially surrounded by land. Bays are *even smaller* and are surrounded by land on three sides. Then there are estuaries, which are enclosed areas where freshwater rivers flow down and meet the ocean.

Those rivers are one of the reasons the ocean is salty. When it rains, tiny bits of minerals from dirt and rocks on land wash down rivers and into the ocean. Two of these minerals—chloride and sodium—combine to make salt. That salt in our oceans was built up over billions of years. Way down at the very bottom of the deep ocean there are also cracks in the earth where undersea volcanoes spew these minerals directly into the water.

There are even animals that live at those volcanoes! So many different parts of the global ocean support life unlike anything we see on land—coral reefs, undersea mountains taller than Mount Everest, forests, and so much more. These are places you'll find ocean animals that have been around since the dinosaurs! Some have no bones. Others are so tiny you can't see them without the help of a microscope. And some never see the sun.

With the three parts of this book (The World's Five Oceans, Spectacular Seas, and All About Oceans) you'll learn cool facts—Did you know the blue whale is the biggest animal to *ever* live, even bigger than the biggest dinosaur?—*and* do fun activities, like word searches and mazes. Are you ready to become an ocean explorer? Dive in!

ARCTIC OCEAN

HUDSON
BAY

BERING
SEA

SARGASSO
SEA

ATLANTIC
OCEAN

PACIFIC
OCEAN

CARIBBEAN
SEA

# Earth's Oceans & Seas

SOUTHERN OCEAN

WEDDELL SEA

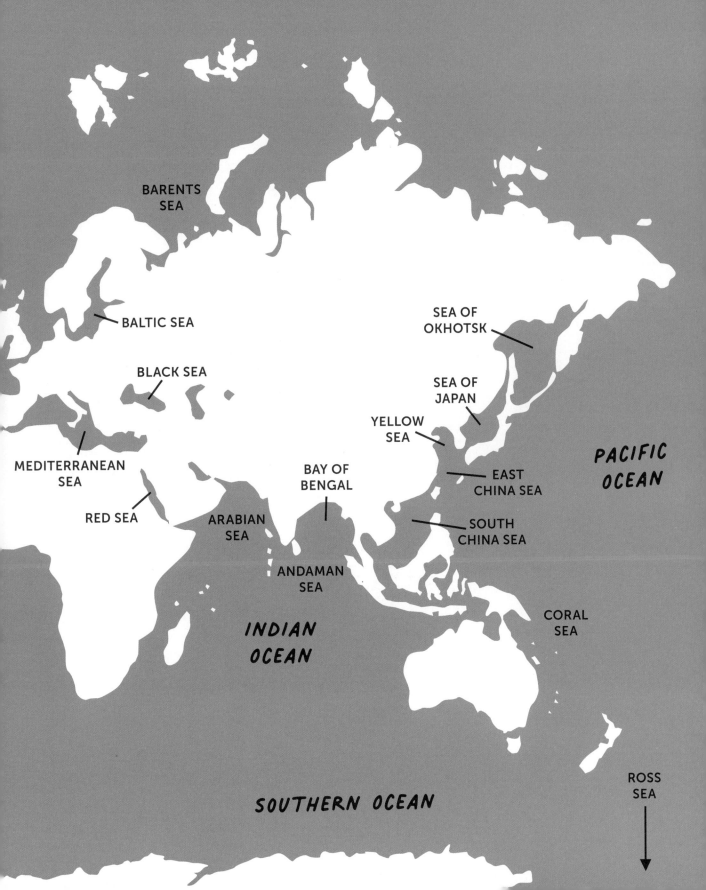

ARCTIC OCEAN

BARENTS
SEA

BALTIC SEA

BLACK SEA

MEDITERRANEAN
SEA

RED SEA

ARABIAN
SEA

BAY OF
BENGAL

ANDAMAN
SEA

SEA OF
OKHOTSK

SEA OF
JAPAN

YELLOW
SEA

EAST
CHINA SEA

SOUTH
CHINA SEA

PACIFIC
OCEAN

CORAL
SEA

INDIAN
OCEAN

SOUTHERN OCEAN

ROSS
SEA

# The World's Five Oceans

Are you ready to explore Planet Ocean? In this section, you'll swim, sail, and dive across Earth's five oceans from the biggest and deepest (the Pacific Ocean) to the smallest and coldest (the Arctic Ocean). Even though they are separated into five named ocean zones, these five oceans are actually one huge global ocean that covers most of our planet. If you took all the land on Earth and added it up, the ocean is still more than six times bigger than that! Not only do the oceans cover 70 percent of the surface of our planet, but did you know that about 97 percent of *all* the water on Earth is ocean water?

Scientists believe life started at the bottom of the ocean, billions of years ago. And we still rely on the ocean. It helps regulate the weather and the temperature and even helps provide the air we breathe. From whales bigger than school buses to plankton so small you can only see them using a microscope, countless different types of animals live in the ocean. In fact, scientists have no idea how many species live in the ocean, since less than 20 percent of the ocean has been mapped, observed, or explored!

# Pacific Ocean

The Pacific Ocean is the Earth's biggest and deepest ocean. It covers one-third of the planet's surface—more than all dry land put together! It's home to the Mariana Trench, the deepest point anywhere on the globe. There are more than 25,000 islands in the Pacific Ocean, and some of those islands were formed by undersea volcanoes. Did you know that the Pacific Ocean has more marine species than any other ocean? Seventy percent of all fish caught in the world are caught in the Pacific.

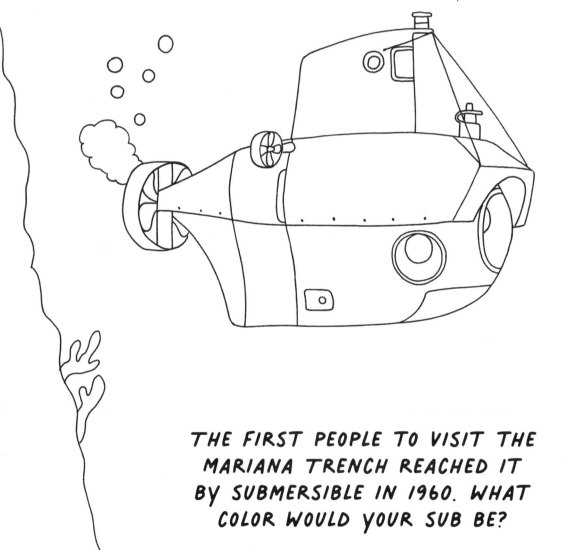

THE FIRST PEOPLE TO VISIT THE
MARIANA TRENCH REACHED IT
BY SUBMERSIBLE IN 1960. WHAT
COLOR WOULD YOUR SUB BE?

Scientists have a word for when there are a lot of different animal species in one place, like there are in the Pacific Ocean. Use the code to learn the word!

___ ___ ___ ___ ___ ___ ___ ___ ___ ___ ___ ___
5   2   8  14  2  10  9  18  4  2  15  13

**KEY**

| 1 | 2 | 3 | 4 | 5 | 6 | 7 | 8 | 9 | 10 | 11 | 12 | 13 |
|---|---|---|---|---|---|---|---|---|----|----|----|----|
| C | I | N | S | B | U | J | O | E | V | M | H | Y |

| 14 | 15 | 16 | 17 | 18 | 19 | 20 | 21 | 22 | 23 | 24 | 25 | 26 |
|----|----|----|----|----|----|----|----|----|----|----|----|----|
| D | T | Z | X | R | A | W | P | K | Q | F | L | G |

HUNDREDS OF COLORFUL ANIMALS LIVE ON CORAL REEFS. THE PACIFIC OCEAN HAS THE MOST CORAL REEFS OF ANY BODY OF WATER ON EARTH. CAN YOU SPOT SIX DIFFERENCES BETWEEN THESE TWO REEFS?

# CAN YOU COMPLETE THIS PACIFIC OCEAN CROSSWORD PUZZLE?

## DOWN

1. The Pacific Ocean isn't the smallest ocean, it's the _____
3. Some of the islands in the Pacific Ocean were formed by _____
4. There are more than 25,000 of these in the Pacific Ocean

## ACROSS

2. The deepest point on Earth is called the _____ Trench
5. Explorers used a _____ to reach the Pacific Ocean's deepest point
6. Seventy percent of all of these are caught in the Pacific

# Atlantic Ocean

Earth's second-biggest ocean is the Atlantic. It separates the Americas from Africa and Europe and covers about 25 percent of the planet's surface. Historians believe it was the first ocean to be crossed by ship and plane. At the bottom of the Atlantic is part of the longest mountain range on Earth—the mid-ocean ridge. Every year the mountains grow and push the land farther and farther apart. That means that the Atlantic gets a tiny bit bigger every year and the Pacific gets a bit smaller!

## CAN YOU FIND SIX PAIRS OF MATCHING WHALES THAT LIVE IN THE ATLANTIC OCEAN?

The world's longest-living vertebrate is named after the Atlantic Ocean's biggest island. Use the code to learn what the animal is!

__ __ __ __ __ __ __ __ __
12  13  23  23  22  9  3  22  26

__ __ __ __ __
18  16  3  13  25

| 1 | 2 | 3 | 4 | 5 | 6 | 7 | 8 | 9 | 10 | 11 | 12 | 13 |
|---|---|---|---|---|---|---|---|---|----|----|----|----|
| J | Q | A | V | F | W | T | B | L | Y | U | G | R |

**KEY**

| 14 | 15 | 16 | 17 | 18 | 19 | 20 | 21 | 22 | 23 | 24 | 25 | 26 |
|----|----|----|----|----|----|----|----|----|----|----|----|----|
| M | I | H | X | S | C | O | Z | N | E | P | K | D |

# THE ATLANTIC IS HOME TO THE WORLD'S MOST-ENDANGERED BIG WHALE SPECIES—THE NORTH ATLANTIC RIGHT WHALE. CONNECT THE DOTS TO REVEAL THE RIGHT WHALE!

# FIND AND CIRCLE THE NAMES OF THESE AMAZING ANIMALS THAT LIVE IN THE ATLANTIC OCEAN.

```
P F S G Q F V T P E M U L O L
Y W Y W Y O F U G E J G A C Z
Q C B U O J A S X T A C E T A
W U X G R R I R N A V O S O B
S E A S P I D E R N E D R P I
L R G X B S U F R A D C O U G
F Y H A W H J J I M H B B S E
R B D M K O G U R S O Q R U Y
D B B X M Z D N T X H M A O E
K O F H L A W X D H Q X H G T
B P G E S N Z G W D J H L M U
I L B F B L U E W H A L E I N
G F X C I G F Z O H E M S I A
D N I G M S X K K Z M Z G U D
U U K S A Q H Z V D V F M B H
```

MANATEE          HARBOR SEAL          DOGFISH

BLUE WHALE          OCTOPUS          SWORDFISH

BIGEYE TUNA          SEA SPIDER

# Indian Ocean

The Indian Ocean is the third-biggest ocean, the warmest ocean (because much of it is near the equator), and the only ocean named after a country (India). Thanks to the warm temperature, it has lots of coral reefs—second only to the Pacific Ocean. The northern part of the Indian Ocean is land-locked; it doesn't reach all the way to the Arctic. And unlike in the Pacific and Atlantic, the ocean currents in the north Indian Ocean don't always move in the same direction—they change with the seasons!

## THE BIGGEST ISLAND IN THE INDIAN OCEAN IS MADAGASCAR. COLOR THE FIVE KINDS OF TURTLES THAT NEST ON MADAGASCAR'S BEACHES.

GREEN TURTLE

OLIVE RIDLEY

LOGGERHEAD

LEATHERBACK

HAWKSBILL

THERE ARE SIX ISLAND NATIONS IN
THE INDIAN OCEAN. TRACE THE
LETTERS TO LEARN THEIR NAMES.

COMOROS

MADAGASCAR

MALDIVES

MAURITIUS

SEYCHELLES

SRI LANKA

WHALE SHARKS IN THE INDIAN OCEAN EAT SMALL SHRIMP, KRILL, AND MICROSCOPIC ANIMALS CALLED PLANKTON. CAN YOU GUIDE THE WHALE SHARK TO ITS FOOD?

START

FINISH

## FILL IN EACH BLANK WITH A WORD FROM THE WORD BANK.

1. Hot or cold? The Indian Ocean is the
   _____ ocean.

2. The northern part of the Indian Ocean is
   _____.

3. Only the Pacific Ocean has more
   _____ than the Indian Ocean.

4. The northern _____ in the Indian
   Ocean change with the seasons.

5. The ocean gets its name from the country of
   _____.

6. It's the _____ biggest ocean
   on Earth.

| CURRENTS | INDIA | THIRD |
| WARMEST | CORAL REEFS | LANDLOCKED |

# Southern Ocean

The Southern Ocean is Earth's "newest" ocean, named by scientists in the year 2000. Before that, the waters around Antarctica (sometimes called the Antarctic Ocean) weren't *officially* an ocean zone. They were just the southernmost parts of the Atlantic, Pacific, and Indian Oceans. It's the only ocean that goes all the way around the globe. Scientists named the Southern Ocean to raise awareness and help protect the amazing animals that live on and around Antarctica—animals like emperor penguins, elephant seals, and orca whales.

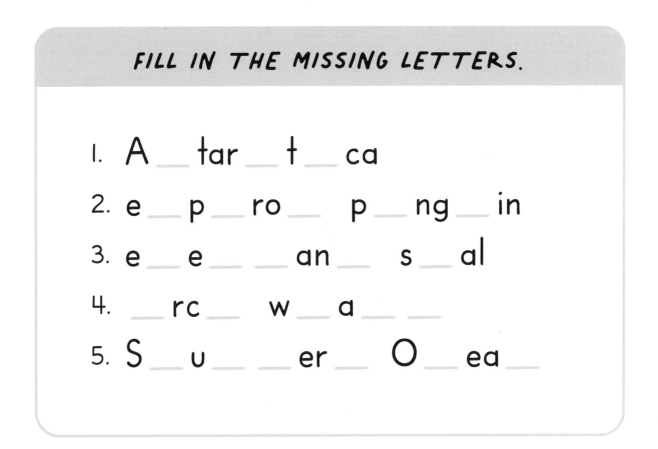

**FILL IN THE MISSING LETTERS.**

1. A __ tar __ t __ ca

2. e __ p __ ro __ p __ ng __ in

3. e __ e __ __ an __ s __ al

4. __ rc __ w __ a __ __

5. S __ __ u __ __ er __ O __ ea __

SIX KINDS OF PENGUINS LIVE ALL OR SOME
OF THE TIME ON ANTARCTICA. CAN YOU MATCH
THE SIX PAIRS OF ANTARCTIC PENGUINS?

# YOU CAN MAKE NEARLY 300 WORDS FROM THE LETTERS IN SOUTHERN, INCLUDING "RUN." LIST EIGHT MORE WORDS HERE.

1. _____

2. _____

3. _____

4. _____

5. _____

6. _____

7. _____

8. _____

# IN 1773, CAPTAIN JAMES COOK AND HIS CREW BECAME THE FIRST TO SAIL WHAT IS NOW THE SOUTHERN OCEAN. CONNECT THE DOTS TO FOLLOW THEIR JOURNEY!

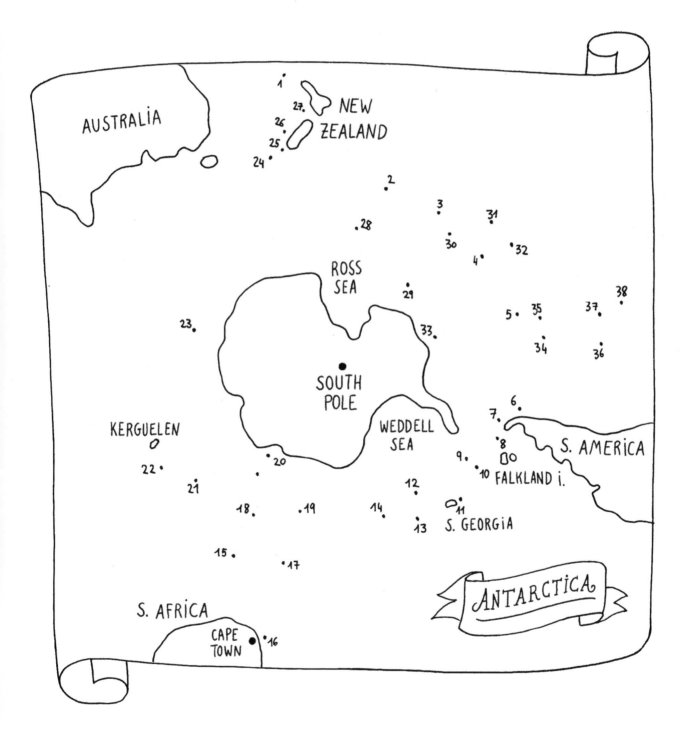

# Arctic Ocean

The smallest ocean in the world is also the coldest and the shallowest. Its waters flow underneath sea ice, ice sheets, and glaciers that make up 10 percent of all the fresh water on Earth. There is a lot of sea ice in the Arctic Ocean; in the winter it grows and covers almost the whole body of water. As the oceans get warmer due to climate change, the sea ice extends a little less every year.

THE ARCTIC IS COMPLETELY DARK FROM OCTOBER UNTIL MARCH. COLOR THE FIRST SPRING SUNRISE!

TRACE THE LETTERS TO LEARN HOW TO WRITE
"ARCTIC OCEAN" IN THE LANGUAGES OF SOME
OF THE COUNTRIES THAT BORDER IT.

NORTHERN ICY OCEAN (FINNISH)

POHJOINEN JÄÄMERI

NORTHERN ICE OCEAN (ICELANDIC)

NORÐUR-ÍSHAF

POLE OCEAN (NORWEGIAN)

POLHAVET

ARCTIC SEA (SWEDISH)

ARKTISKA HAVET

NORTHERN ICE-COVERED OCEAN (RUSSIAN)

SEVERNOGO
LEDOVITNOGO OKEAN

# WALRUSES SPEND MOST OF THEIR LIVES IN AND AROUND THE ARCTIC OCEAN. HERE'S HOW TO DRAW ONE.

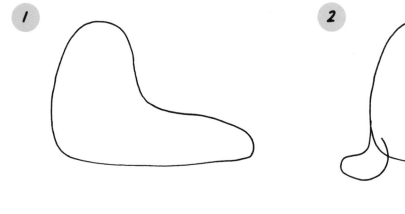

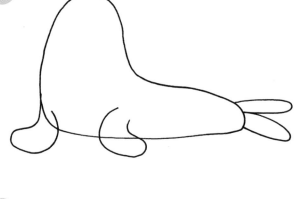

## NOW DRAW ONE ON YOUR OWN!

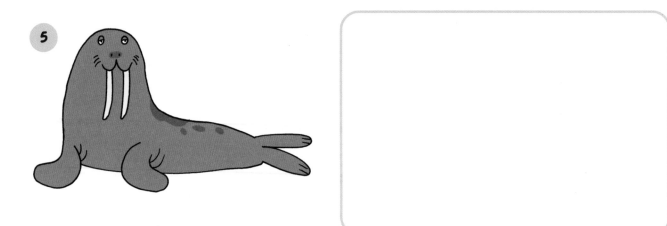

# FIND AND CIRCLE THE NAMES OF THESE ANIMALS THAT CAN BE FOUND IN THE ARCTIC OCEAN.

```
W Z N F E U S S D E Y L H S U X
T U A K B P Y N F E L M Q X H
X A K G O O A P B H A L X A Q
O L L G U R E I O P G R R L Q
H W O X W L V M W C E P B Y L
B N L H I L E J H C S F A X Y
G A A E Q E J B E E P D R M M
D L P U F F I N A N O L C W A
S O R F E V W L D L L N G S R
R U I V Q H J N W D A I N E P
G H R S A B A K H O R C I I B
T S S L J C J A A Y B Y K Z N
F M O G A P L B L S E K Q B L
Z C Z H L W Z U E S A U Z A O
C J X O W F P H R R R M A X I
```

POLAR BEAR       NARWHAL          PUFFIN

WALRUS           BOWHEAD WHALE    KING CRAB

BELUGA           HARP SEAL

# Spectacular Seas

For hundreds of years, people called the global ocean "the seven seas." Lots of people use "sea" and "ocean" to mean the same thing, but they *are* different, at least geographically. They both have salt water, but geographers (the scientists who study the surface of the Earth) say there are two big differences. First, seas are smaller than oceans. And second, most of the time they're partially enclosed by land. There's no single meaning for what exactly makes a sea, but they're usually located where the land and the ocean meet.

"Usually" is an important word here because some seas don't meet that definition at all. The Caspian Sea, found between Asia and Europe, is completely landlocked and bigger than Japan! Other seas aren't bordered by land but by special currents that move through the water, or by lines on a map.

Since there isn't one definition of what a sea is, scientists don't agree on how many seas there are in the world, but it's close to 50. In this section you'll learn about 20 of Earth's most spectacular seas, picked for their size and importance to the people and animals around them. They're organized by ocean (biggest to smallest) and then alphabetically. Turn the page and start sailing!

# Bering Sea

Located between Alaska and Russia, the Bering Sea connects the Arctic Ocean and Pacific Ocean. Its narrowest point—the Bering Strait—is only 55 miles wide. Thousands of years ago, during the last ice age, the water level in the Bering Strait dropped so low that a land bridge formed in the strait. Early humans and animals used it to migrate from Asia to North America on foot! The Bering Sea is one of the most productive fishing grounds in the world. The United States alone catches about $1 billion worth of seafood there every year.

### YOU CAN MAKE 254 WORDS OUT OF THE LETTERS IN BERING SEA, INCLUDING "BEAR." CAN YOU LIST EIGHT MORE?

1. _____

2. _____

3. _____

4. _____

5. _____

6. _____

7. _____

8. _____

# CAN YOU SPOT SIX DIFFERENCES BETWEEN THESE TWO FISHING BOATS?

# Coral Sea

The Coral Sea is in the southern Pacific Ocean near Australia. It's named for all the coral reefs in its waters, including the largest coral reef system in the world—the Great Barrier Reef. The Great Barrier Reef stretches more than 1,400 miles long and is made up of thousands of reefs and 900 islands. It's so big it can be seen by astronauts on the International Space Station! Since corals are alive, the Great Barrier Reef is the largest living structure on the entire planet.

## CAN YOU UNSCRAMBLE THESE CORAL SEA WORDS?

1. LROAC FERSE _____

_____

2. CCFIAIP ANEOC _____

_____

3. LAAUASRTI _____

4. STORANTUAS _____

5. LSANDIS _____

# CORAL REEFS ARE SOME OF THE MOST COLORFUL PLACES ON EARTH. USE THE KEY BELOW TO COLOR THE GREAT BARRIER REEF.

1 PINK

2 BLUE

3 GRAY

4 ORANGE

5 YELLOW

6 RED

# East China Sea

The East China Sea gets its name from its location—east of China. Even though it's called the East China Sea, people from China, Japan, Taiwan, and South Korea all share the waters. It's an active area for fishing many different types of animals, including tuna, sardines, shrimp, squid, mackerel, and milkfish. For a sea, it's pretty shallow, with nearly 75 percent of it less than 660 feet deep. (The average depth of the global ocean is 12,100 feet.) The longest river in Asia, the Yangtze River, drains into the East China Sea.

MOUNT PUTUO IN THE EAST CHINA SEA IS A SACRED SITE IN THE CHINESE BUDDHIST RELIGION. COLOR SOME THINGS YOU'D SEE ON MOUNT PUTUO.

# FIND AND CIRCLE THE NAMES OF THESE ANIMALS THAT CAN BE FOUND IN THE EAST CHINA SEA.

```
G U B M D Z Y P W I F S V X E
S K E G C T D H C D E G M B M
P M I R H S D U F M B J D H B
G V S Y U E F O O S O E I S E
M A E R B A E S F C W C O I A
Z Z S E N I D R A S F K O F W
F S R E K A O R C Q I Y T K A
W K C Z C T D C X T F D L L F
U D T X D M Z P H T I V O I N
O M A C K E R E L U C N X M W
D Y R Y F C G Z Q N Y X L G S
Z L E N G D O S P A V T L R R
M R U K M I R M A T X B U C J
R Y A C A T P R O V H E P G D
G J E U D N Y I L D F W W P F
```

TUNA             SQUID            SEA BREAM

SARDINES         MACKEREL         CROAKERS

SHRIMP           MILKFISH

# Sea of Japan

North of the East China Sea, the Sea of Japan separates Japan from North and South Korea and mainland Russia from Sakhalin Island (Russia's largest island). Yamato Bank is an underwater mountain range in the center of the sea that is just over 1,000 feet deep at its shallowest. The Sea of Japan is mostly cut off from the Pacific Ocean, which means it has almost no tides! It's rich in wildlife and home to more than 3,500 animal species, including dolphins, seals, and many different types of whales. In China, the ancient name for the area was "Sea of Whales."

THE SEA OF JAPAN IS NAMED FOR THE COUNTRY OF JAPAN, WHICH IS FAMOUS FOR ITS SUSHI (RAW FISH WITH RICE). CAN YOU MATCH SIX PAIRS OF SUSHI?

# CAN YOU COMPLETE THIS SEA OF JAPAN CROSSWORD PUZZLE?

## DOWN

1. The Sea of Japan is this direction from the East China Sea

2. Ancient China's name for the area was the Sea of _____

3. The Sea of Japan is part of this ocean

## ACROSS

4. The Sea of Japan is home to more than 3,500 types of this

5. Russia's largest island is named _____

6. The Sea of Japan has almost none of these

# Sea of Okhotsk

The Sea of Okhotsk, off the eastern coast of Russia, is one of the richest marine ecosystems in the world. That means lots of different types of animals live there, including the largest sea eagle in the world—the Steller's sea eagle. It has a wingspan bigger than 6.6 feet! There are only about 7,500 Steller's sea eagles left, and they only live around the Sea of Okhotsk. The sea, which forms giant frozen ice sheets in the winter, is also home to tufted puffins, ringed seals, and bowhead whales.

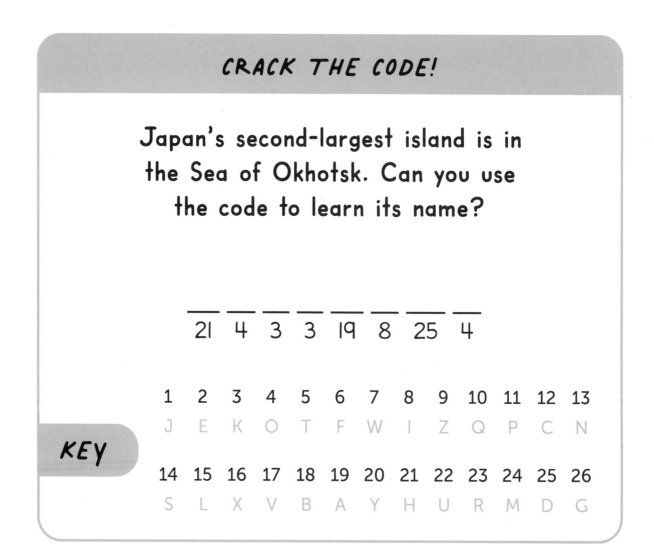

CRACK THE CODE!

Japan's second-largest island is in the Sea of Okhotsk. Can you use the code to learn its name?

__ __ __ __ __ __ __ __
21  4  3  3  19  8  25  4

KEY

| 1 | 2 | 3 | 4 | 5 | 6 | 7 | 8 | 9 | 10 | 11 | 12 | 13 |
|---|---|---|---|---|---|---|---|---|----|----|----|----|
| J | E | K | O | T | F | W | I | Z | Q  | P  | C  | N  |

| 14 | 15 | 16 | 17 | 18 | 19 | 20 | 21 | 22 | 23 | 24 | 25 | 26 |
|----|----|----|----|----|----|----|----|----|----|----|----|----|
| S  | L  | X  | V  | B  | A  | Y  | H  | U  | R  | M  | D  | G  |

PEOPLE CALL THE SEA OF OKHOTSK A "BIRD LOVER'S PARADISE." HOW MANY BIRDS CAN YOU FIND?

# South China Sea

The South China Sea is bordered by Brunei, China, Indonesia, Malaysia, the Philippines, Singapore, Taiwan, and Vietnam. For centuries, the sea has been a hugely important area for traders, who used to transport fine goods like ceramics, silks, and spices through it. Now more than one-third of the world's shipping passes through the South China Sea—that's more than $3 trillion worth of goods that travel through it by ship every year!

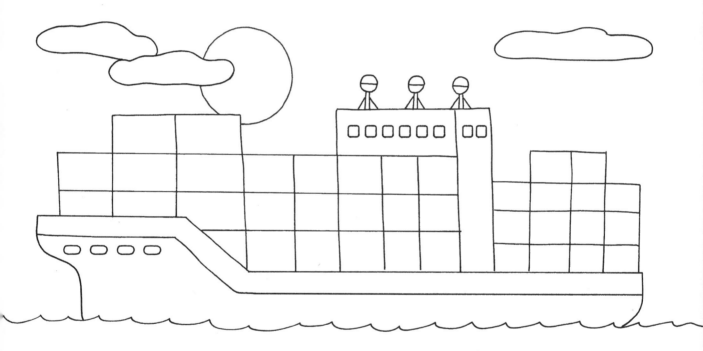

**SHIPS AS BIG AS SKYSCRAPERS PASS THROUGH THE SOUTH CHINA SEA EVERY DAY! COLOR THE CONTAINER SHIP.**

TRACE THE NAMES OF THE COUNTRIES THAT BORDER THE SOUTH CHINA SEA.

BRUNEI

CHINA

INDONESIA

MALAYSIA

THE PHILIPPINES

SINGAPORE

TAIWAN

VIETNAM

# Yellow Sea

The Yellow Sea separates North and South Korea from China. Its name comes from its color. Where silty rivers from China run into the sea, the area turns a yellowish brown. Every year 1.6 *billion* tons of sediment empty into the sea. More than 600 million people live near the Yellow Sea—that's nearly 10 percent of all the people on Earth! Pollution and overfishing have caused problems for the animals that live in the Yellow Sea, but scientists around the world are working to make it healthy again.

### A JUNK IS A TYPE OF CHINESE SAILING SHIP THAT OFTEN SAILED THE YELLOW SEA. CAN YOU MATCH SIX JUNKS?

## FILL IN EACH BLANK WITH A WORD FROM THE WORD BANK.

1. Every year 1.6 billion tons of _____ empty into the Yellow Sea.

2. Nearly 10 percent of all the _____ on Earth live near the Yellow Sea.

3. The Yellow Sea separates North and South Korea from _____.

4. Silty _____ empty into the Yellow Sea.

5. The Yellow Sea gets its name from its _____.

6. Around the world, _____ are working hard to make the Yellow Sea healthy again.

| COLOR | SEDIMENT | PEOPLE |
| CHINA | SCIENTISTS | RIVERS |

# Baltic Sea

The Baltic Sea is sometimes called an "arm" of the Atlantic because of the way it branches off from the ocean (and its narrow shape *does* look like an arm). Lots of fresh water from the surrounding rivers drains into it, making the sea much less salty than the ocean. The scientific word for that mixed water is "brackish." The Baltic Sea is the largest inland brackish sea in the world. In the eighth century, Vikings started to sail the Baltic Sea for trade and exploration; it's still vital for trade today.

## FIND AND CIRCLE THE NAMES OF THE COUNTRIES THAT BORDER THE BALTIC SEA.

DENMARK

ESTONIA

FINLAND

GERMANY

LATVIA

LITHUANIA

POLAND

RUSSIA

SWEDEN

```
A N J U X M O M T Y V R T W E
K K L F I M R E P P O S N W V
K R F Q A I S S U R V J R F F
R A F F D G E R M A N Y D V X
Q M I L I B C D P N M T W P U
G N Q X X P L C S P A G X L F
H E O Y Z P V D H I M L D M X
W D X K K J W N N K O A Y S E
S D F Q S V A A P P W T H J Y
L W L I J I U L L X Y V D M R
X W P Q N H U O L Y L I F W R
Q Q P O T L U P W J H A D W K
S G T I I K A P V E J S I P F
Z S L D X I J N S F J H O A T
E B W B B S W E D E N H F F S
```

# CONNECT THE DOTS TO REVEAL A VIKING SHIP!

# Black Sea

The Black Sea is one of the largest inland bodies of water on Earth. Located where Eastern Europe meets Western Asia, it's as big as California. There are about 180 kinds of fish in the Black Sea, but those fish can only live near the surface. The bottom layers of the Black Sea are a "dead zone"—there's almost no oxygen and nothing can live there. The Black Sea has been important for trade for thousands of years. In 2018, scientists found a Greek merchant ship at the bottom of the sea that's 2,400 years old!

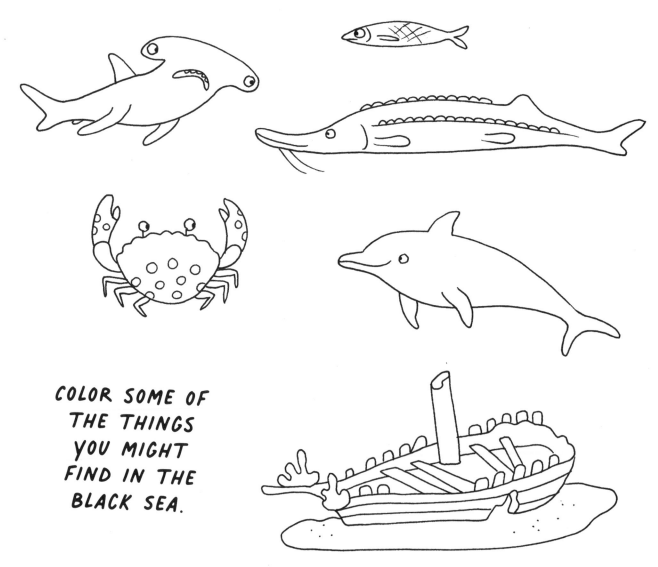

COLOR SOME OF THE THINGS YOU MIGHT FIND IN THE BLACK SEA.

# ARE THESE FACTS TRUE OR FALSE?
## CIRCLE THE RIGHT ANSWER.

1. Fish can live anywhere in the Black Sea.

   TRUE   FALSE

2. There's almost no oxygen at the bottom of the Black Sea.

   TRUE   FALSE

3. People have sailed the Black Sea for thousands of years.

   TRUE   FALSE

4. There are only 50 types of fish in the Black Sea.

   TRUE   FALSE

5. The oldest shipwreck in the Black Sea is 500 years old.

   TRUE   FALSE

# Caribbean Sea

The Caribbean Sea is located between the coasts of Central and South America, the Gulf of Mexico, and the West Indies islands. Its name comes from the Carib, the native people who lived on the Caribbean islands hundreds of years ago. The Caribbean Sea is home to coral reefs, mangrove forests, and more than 1,400 kinds of fish and marine mammals, including tiger sharks, manatees, sea turtles, moray eels, giant manta rays, and parrotfish. The Mesoamerican Reef, the world's second-largest coral reef, is in the Caribbean Sea.

**CAN YOU FIND SIX MATCHING PAIRS OF CARIBBEAN SEA ANIMALS?**

# CRACK THE CODE!

The deepest spot in the Caribbean
Sea is more than 25,000 feet deep.
Use the code to learn its name.

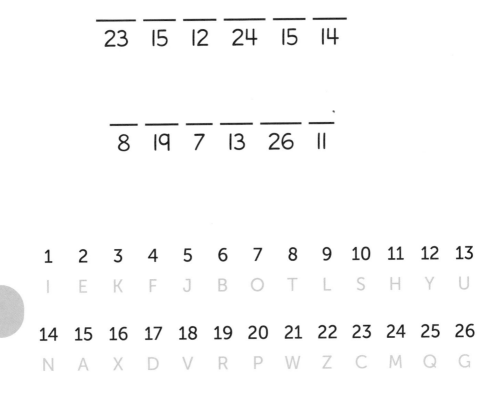

| | | | | | |
|---|---|---|---|---|---|
| 23 | 15 | 12 | 24 | 15 | 14 |

| | | | | | |
|---|---|---|---|---|---|
| 8 | 19 | 7 | 13 | 26 | 11 |

| 1 | 2 | 3 | 4 | 5 | 6 | 7 | 8 | 9 | 10 | 11 | 12 | 13 |
|---|---|---|---|---|---|---|---|---|---|---|---|---|
| I | E | K | F | J | B | O | T | L | S | H | Y | U |

**KEY**

| 14 | 15 | 16 | 17 | 18 | 19 | 20 | 21 | 22 | 23 | 24 | 25 | 26 |
|---|---|---|---|---|---|---|---|---|---|---|---|---|
| N | A | X | D | V | R | P | W | Z | C | M | Q | G |

# Mediterranean Sea

The Mediterranean Sea is the only sea on Earth that touches three continents—Europe to the north, Africa to the south, and Asia to the east. Twenty-two countries touch the Mediterranean! It's sometimes called "the cradle of civilization," and throughout history, people have relied on it for food, trade, exploration, and to wage war. The Strait of Gibraltar, where the Mediterranean meets the Atlantic Ocean, is only eight miles wide at its narrowest. Six million years ago the Mediterranean was a dry desert!

### YOU CAN MAKE 549 WORDS FROM THE LETTERS IN MEDITERRANEAN, INCLUDING "TEA." CAN YOU LIST EIGHT MORE?

1. _____

2. _____

3. _____

4. _____

5. _____

6. _____

7. _____

8. _____

# SPOT SIX DIFFERENCES BETWEEN THESE TWO PICTURES OF SICILY, THE BIGGEST ISLAND IN THE MEDITERRANEAN SEA.

# Sargasso Sea

Located in the Atlantic Ocean near Bermuda, the Sargasso Sea is bordered by four ocean currents (called a gyre) instead of land. These four huge currents rotate clockwise with the Sargasso Sea in the middle to form the North Atlantic Gyre. The sea gets its name from *Sargassum*, a brown seaweed that floats on the surface of the water thanks to those currents. Unfortunately, the currents mean other things are trapped on the surface, too, including an enormous floating pile of trash known as the North Atlantic garbage patch.

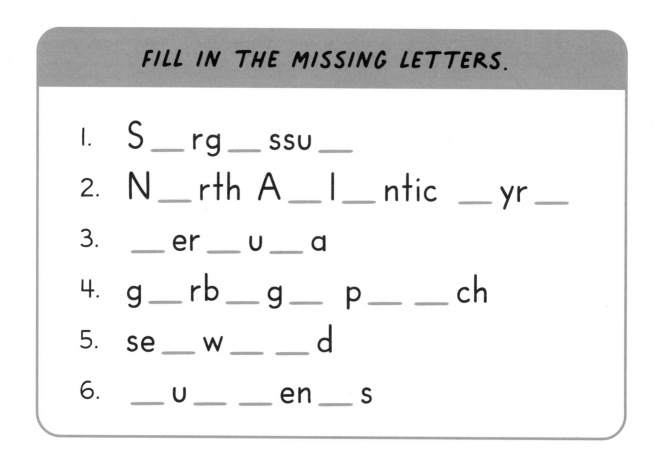

### FILL IN THE MISSING LETTERS.

1. S __ rg __ ssu __

2. N __ rth A __ l __ ntic __ yr __

3. __ er __ u __ a

4. g __ rb __ g __ p __ __ ch

5. se __ w __ __ d

6. __ u __ __ en __ s

BERMUDA IS THE ONLY ISLAND
IN THE SARGASSO SEA. COLOR
WHAT YOU CAN SEE IN BERMUDA.

# Andaman Sea

The Andaman Sea is in the northwest Indian Ocean, between Myanmar and Thailand. The sea gets its name from the Andaman Islands—a chain of islands on its western border. Trading boats have sailed the Andaman Sea since ancient times, when it was an early trade route between India and China. Even now it's a major shipping route between those two countries. The bottom of the Andaman Sea has two tectonic plates (huge, moving parts of the Earth's crust), so the area has lots of earthquakes!

## UNSCRAMBLE THESE ANDAMAN SEA WORDS.

1. NIDAIN CAENO _____

2. NOCTCETI _____

3. LDIAATHN _____

4. MNAAAND LNIDSSA _____

5. ADRET ORUET _____

6. QKRTAHESEUA _____

# THE ONLY ACTIVE VOLCANO IN THE REGION IS ON BARREN ISLAND IN THE ANDAMAN SEA. USE THE KEY TO COLOR BARREN ISLAND.

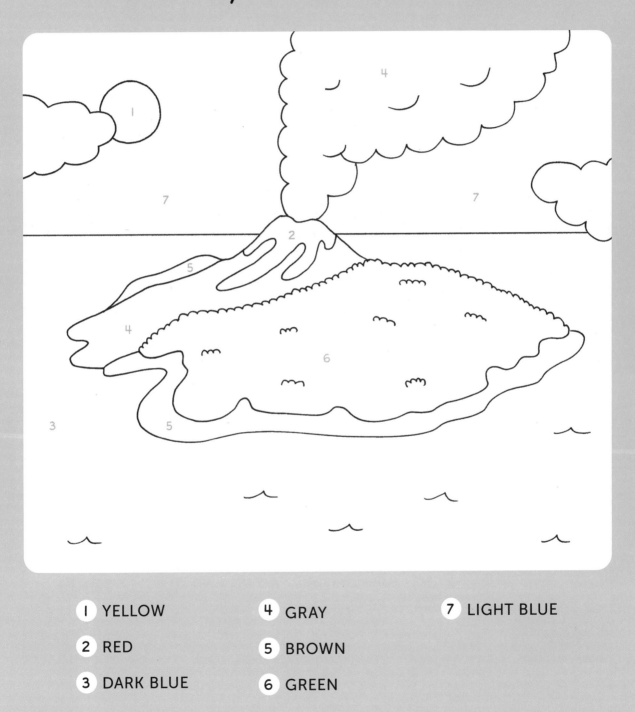

1 YELLOW    4 GRAY    7 LIGHT BLUE

2 RED    5 BROWN

3 DARK BLUE    6 GREEN

# Arabian Sea

The Arabian Sea is located in the northwest Indian Ocean. It was named after the Arabian Peninsula to its west. Historians believe that traders sailed along the coast of the Arabian Sea as far back as 3000 BCE—that's more than 5,000 years ago! The Arabian Sea has one of the world's largest "dead zones," an area of water with so little oxygen that almost no animals can survive. The Arabian Sea's dead zone has the lowest levels of oxygen in the world.

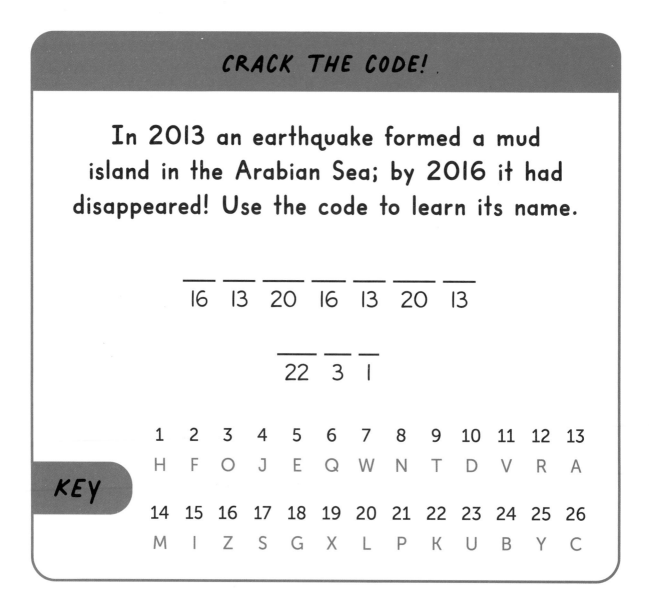

## CRACK THE CODE!

In 2013 an earthquake formed a mud island in the Arabian Sea; by 2016 it had disappeared! Use the code to learn its name.

__ __ __ __ __ __ __
16  13  20  16  13  20  13

__ __ __
22   3   1

| 1 | 2 | 3 | 4 | 5 | 6 | 7 | 8 | 9 | 10 | 11 | 12 | 13 |
|---|---|---|---|---|---|---|---|---|----|----|----|----|
| H | F | O | J | E | Q | W | N | T | D | V | R | A |

| 14 | 15 | 16 | 17 | 18 | 19 | 20 | 21 | 22 | 23 | 24 | 25 | 26 |
|----|----|----|----|----|----|----|----|----|----|----|----|----|
| M | I | Z | S | G | X | L | P | K | U | B | Y | C |

**KEY**

THERE ARE FEWER THAN 100 HUMPBACK WHALES IN THE ARABIAN SEA. LEARN HOW TO DRAW AN ARABIAN HUMPBACK WHALE.

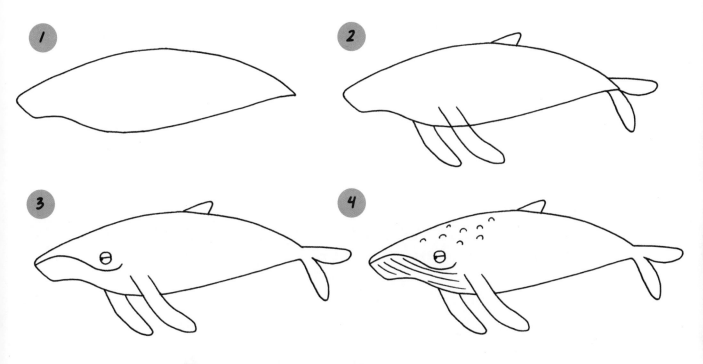

NOW DRAW ONE ON YOUR OWN!

# Bay of Bengal

The Bay of Bengal, located in the northeast Indian Ocean to the east of India, is home to hundreds of different types of plants and animals. On its shores is Cox's Bazar, the longest sea beach in the world, and the Sundarbans, one of Earth's largest mangrove forests. Deep below the surface, it's just as interesting. The "Swatch of No Ground" is an 8.6-mile-deep trench. It's part of the Bengal Fan—a large underwater ravine caused by river currents.

### YOU CAN MAKE MORE THAN 183 WORDS OUT OF THE LETTERS IN BAY OF BENGAL, INCLUDING "BEG." CAN YOU COME UP WITH EIGHT MORE?

1. _____

2. _____

3. _____

4. _____

5. _____

6. _____

7. _____

8. _____

THE SUNDARBANS MANGROVE FOREST IS HOME TO LOTS OF DIFFERENT ANIMALS. CAN YOU FIND A CROCODILE, AN EAGLE, A TIGER, AN OTTER, A SAWFISH, AND A SEA TURTLE?

# Red Sea

The Red Sea is one of the saltiest bodies of water on Earth. It's located between Saudi Arabia and Yemen on the east and Egypt, Sudan, Eritrea, and Djibouti on the west. It is a rich and healthy ecosystem with more than 1,200 species of fish, 10 percent of which are found *only* in the Red Sea—nowhere else in the world. The sea is popular with scuba divers. Some of the coral reefs along the coast are more than 5,000 years old!

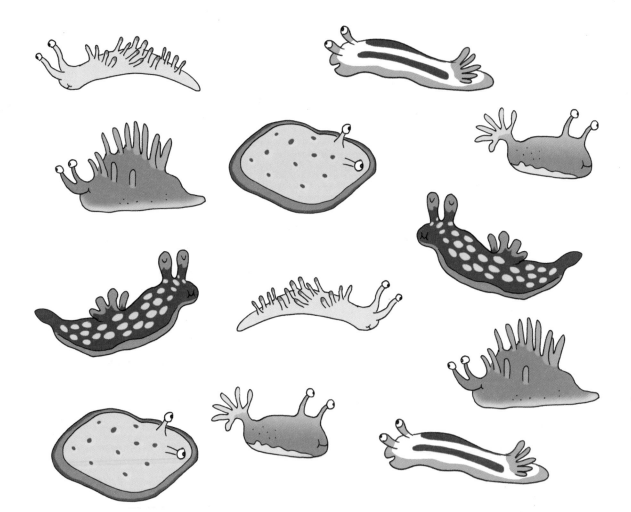

THE RED SEA IS HOME TO MORE THAN 175 TYPES OF COLORFUL SEA SLUGS CALLED "NUDIBRANCHS." CAN YOU FIND SIX MATCHING PAIRS?

# FIND AND CIRCLE THE NAMES OF THESE ANIMALS THAT CAN BE FOUND IN THE RED SEA.

```
T  S  A  P  E  X  S  G  I  S  U  W  U  E  W
Z  F  O  R  O  H  Y  R  Q  B  D  Y  A  A  R
K  R  F  H  J  Q  M  O  T  Z  F  L  N  G  U
L  H  R  A  B  V  A  U  S  I  U  R  G  L  W
D  O  X  Y  D  F  I  P  E  Z  J  O  E  E  M
Q  A  L  R  O  U  P  E  A  T  C  A  L  R  X
U  N  E  W  P  A  C  R  H  T  G  F  F  A  S
C  E  A  R  L  B  P  A  O  P  E  F  I  Y  R
Q  M  L  N  W  I  X  P  R  Q  S  M  S  U  E
D  O  F  P  N  X  U  B  S  R  S  X  H  Q  A
B  N  M  G  G  S  Y  E  E  K  A  Q  N  X  F
R  E  K  J  M  P  L  O  K  A  R  B  Z  U  C
L  W  C  Q  W  I  V  W  C  Y  W  D  Y  X  X
C  S  P  K  G  N  V  C  A  P  U  K  W  C  Y
D  W  R  B  U  V  I  Z  I  O  U  A  X  O  S
```

| BARRACUDA | EAGLE RAY | OCTOPUS |
|-----------|-----------|---------|
| ANGELFISH | GROUPER | SEAHORSE |
| WRASSE | ANEMONE | |

# Ross Sea

Tucked way down next to Antarctica, Ross Sea is the southernmost sea on Earth. It's named after British explorer James Clark Ross, who discovered the sea during an Antarctic expedition in 1841. Part of the Ross Sea is covered by the Ross Ice Shelf, the largest floating sheet of ice attached to a landmass in Antarctica. Ross Sea is home to birds like penguins and petrels; at least 10 kinds of mammals, including minke whales and leopard seals; nearly 100 types of fish; and more than 1,000 kinds of invertebrates (animals with no bones).

## FILL IN EACH BLANK WITH A WORD FROM THE WORD BANK.

1. Ross Sea was discovered in _____.

2. Animals with no bones are called _____.

3. The _____ is the largest ice shelf in Antarctica.

4. Ross Sea is the _____ sea on Earth.

5 The sea is named after _____.

6. There are nearly _____ types of fish in the Ross Sea.

| | | |
|---|---|---|
| JAMES CLARK ROSS | 100 | SOUTHERNMOST |
| ROSS ICE SHELF | 1841 | INVERTEBRATES |

IN 2007, FISHERMEN IN THE
ROSS SEA CAUGHT A 33-FOOT-LONG,
1,000-POUND ANIMAL. CONNECT THE
DOTS TO SEE THE COLOSSAL SQUID!

6

7

.32

31

5

8

.9

33

4

.10

3

1

2

.30

11

12

29.

13

14

28

15

27

16

20   .18

26 .  24      17

22

19

25

21

23

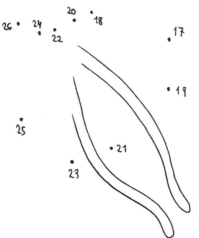

# Weddell Sea

The shores and waters of Antarctica's Weddell Sea are home to seals, whales, and a colony of more than 200,000 Adélie penguins. Named after British sailor James Weddell, who discovered the sea in 1823, the Weddell Sea is full of dangerous currents, winds, and sea ice. In 1915, the famous Antarctic explorer Ernest Shackleton's ship, the *Endurance*, was trapped and crushed by ice in the Weddell Sea, stranding his team of explorers for nearly two years. Scientists found the *Endurance* still mostly intact on the seafloor in 2020!

## MATCH THE CLUES ON THE LEFT SIDE WITH THE CORRECT ANSWERS ON THE RIGHT SIDE.

1. Person the sea is named after
2. Name of the famous shipwreck
3. There is a colony of more than 200,000 of these
4. Continent nearest to the Weddell Sea
5. This traps boats in the Weddell Sea
6. Year the sea was discovered

A. Adélie penguins

B. sea ice

C. *Endurance*

D. Antarctica

E. 1823

F. James Weddell

# Barents Sea

Located off the coasts of Russia and Norway, Barents Sea is the largest sea of the Arctic Ocean. In the Middle Ages, the Russians and the Vikings called it the Murman Sea. The warmer waters of the Atlantic Ocean currents meet the cold Arctic Ocean here; these mixing currents mean the Barents Sea is full of sea life. This sea has the world's largest population of codfish, and it's an important feeding ground for more than 20 species of marine mammals, including narwhals, orcas, and blue whales.

## FIND AND CIRCLE THE NAMES OF THESE ANIMALS THAT CAN BE FOUND IN THE BARENTS SEA.

NARWHAL

ORCA

MINKE WHALE

HARP SEAL

POLAR BEAR

WALRUS

PORPOISE

PUFFIN

```
A S M E X H J E Y D A B G G I
Q K X A Y Z U U S T K C W Z D
E J N A R W H A L W L P R R B
F Y Y H J O J N P B U U V O D
E Z X C K R L H O Q Q F S C G
A T D X D Y T C L C F F C G Y
R P G Z V K Z Q A V U I N G X
V Z J E S I O P R O P N D L H
X H E K S C B H B Z G J E A C
L N S S U B T I E M V D S E X
D P T J R G M B A H A J V S Z
C G K G L X F K R L V P G P P
O F Q A A E G D M P L M K R S
B J J R W P G K H Y Q Q X A I
G M I N K E W H A L E N C H P
```

BARENTS SEA IS SO FAR NORTH THAT
YOU CAN SEE THE NORTHERN LIGHTS!
COLOR BY NUMBER TO SEE THE MAGIC.

1 DARK BLUE     3 LIME GREEN     5 DARK GRAY

2 LIGHT PURPLE  4 GRAY           6 PINK

# Hudson Bay

Even though it's called a "bay," Hudson Bay is a sea of the Arctic Ocean. It's nestled into Canada and touches four Canadian regions—Nunavut, Manitoba, Ontario, and Quebec. Hudson Bay is the second-biggest body of water with "bay" in the name, after the Bay of Bengal in the Indian Ocean. Hudson Bay is home to seals, polar bears, walruses, bowhead whales, and beluga whales. Every summer, 55,000 belugas migrate to the Hudson Bay from the Arctic Ocean to feed, shed their skin, and give birth!

## UNSCRAMBLE THESE HUDSON BAY WORDS.

1. TNAUNUV _____

2. GBLUASE _____

3. CTCRAI NAOEC _____

4. SRULWESA _____

5. LAOPR AESBR _____

6. CBEUQE _____

# CAN YOU SPOT SIX DIFFERENCES IN THESE TWO PICTURES OF BELUGA WHALES IN HUDSON BAY?

# All About Oceans

Take a deep breath and then thank the ocean. More than half of the air you breathe comes from ocean plants like seaweed and tiny algae called phytoplankton. They turn carbon dioxide into oxygen—what you breathe. Are you ready to learn all about the amazing plants and animals that call the oceans home—and more? In this part of the book, you'll find out about the biggest whales and the ocean's microscopic organisms, learn what lives under the waves and how tides work, meet the animals that live in coral reefs and in underwater forests, explore the ocean's deepest trenches and find animals that have evolved to live their lives without ever seeing the sun, and find "living fossils" that haven't changed since dinosaurs roamed the Earth. You'll discover shipwrecks and learn about the explorers who bravely began sailing the sea, even though some people feared they might sail off the edge of the Earth. There are so many exciting things to learn about our oceans, things that impact everyone on the planet—even you!

# Magnificent Mammals

To be a mammal, an animal has to have hair or fur, be warm-blooded, and give birth to live babies instead of laying eggs. There are 130 different kinds of mammals that live in the ocean (called marine mammals). You've probably heard of dolphins, whales, walruses, orcas, and seals. But there are also "sea cows" and narwhals. Sea otters and polar bears also count as marine mammals because they rely on the ocean to survive. Mammals thrive in every part of the global ocean—even the cold Antarctic!

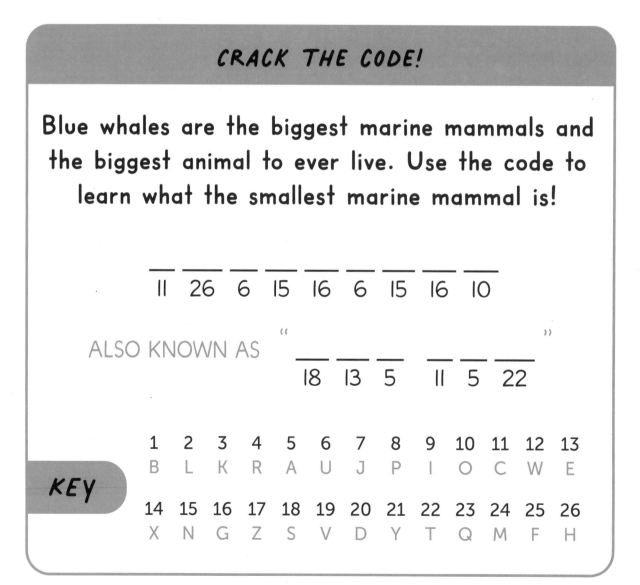

## CRACK THE CODE!

Blue whales are the biggest marine mammals and the biggest animal to ever live. Use the code to learn what the smallest marine mammal is!

___ ___ ___ ___ ___ ___ ___ ___ ___
11  26  6  15  16  6  15  16  10

ALSO KNOWN AS  " ___ ___ ___  ___ ___ ___ "
                18  13  5   11  5  22

KEY

| 1 | 2 | 3 | 4 | 5 | 6 | 7 | 8 | 9 | 10 | 11 | 12 | 13 |
|---|---|---|---|---|---|---|---|---|----|----|----|----|
| B | L | K | R | A | U | J | P | I | O  | C  | W  | E  |

| 14 | 15 | 16 | 17 | 18 | 19 | 20 | 21 | 22 | 23 | 24 | 25 | 26 |
|----|----|----|----|----|----|----|----|----|----|----|----|----|
| X  | N  | G  | Z  | S  | V  | D  | Y  | T  | Q  | M  | F  | H  |

ORCAS, SOMETIMES CALLED "KILLER WHALES," AREN'T
TECHNICALLY WHALES. THEY'RE ACTUALLY THE LARGEST
DOLPHIN SPECIES! LEARN TO DRAW A BREACHING ORCA.

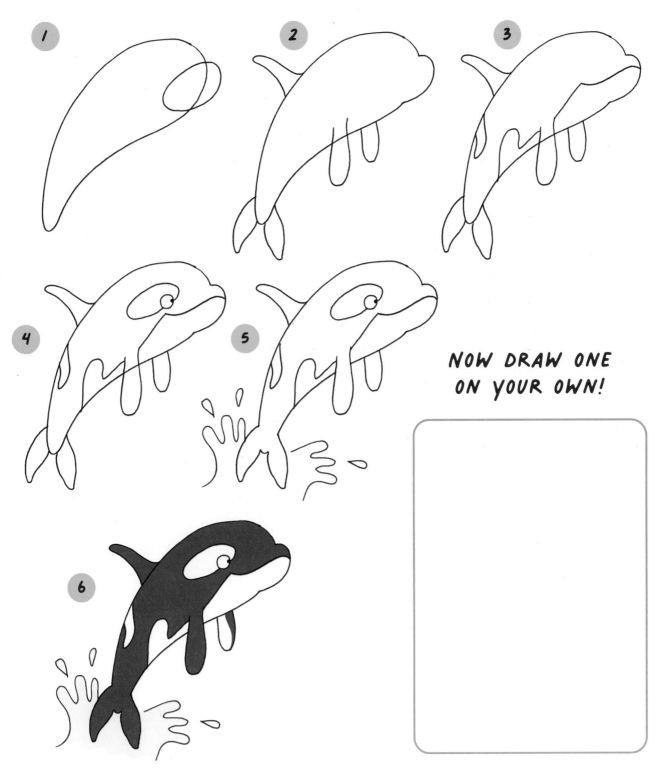

NOW DRAW ONE
ON YOUR OWN!

# Fascinating Fish

If someone told you to draw a fish, would you draw a shark? You could, because sharks are a type of fish! Great white sharks can reach 20 feet long, but they're not the biggest fish in the world. That's the whale shark, which is named for its size (60 feet long) and how it eats (filter feeding). Greenland sharks can live for 500 years. Sharks and their stingray cousins don't have any bones. Instead, their skeletons are made of cartilage, like what's in your nose. The largest bony fish in the world is the ocean sunfish—the *Mola mola*.

**THERE ARE ABOUT 400 SPECIES OF SHARKS IN THE OCEAN. CAN YOU MATCH SIX SHARK PAIRS?**

# HOW MUCH DID YOU LEARN? COMPLETE THIS FISHY CROSSWORD AND FIND OUT!

## DOWN

1. Stingrays don't have any _____
2. Shark skeletons are made of _____
3. The _____ shark can live up to 500 years

## ACROSS

4. _____ sharks can be up to 60 feet long!
5. Sharks and stingrays are types of _____
6. The largest bony fish in the world

# Birds, Big and Small

The most famous seabirds are penguins. Many people think all penguins live near the South Pole, but only 6 of the 17 species live on Antarctica. Most live off the coasts of Africa and South America. The Galápagos penguin is the only species that lives north of the equator. Another well-known seabird is the puffin. Sometimes called "sea parrots" because of their bright beaks, puffins can dive nearly 200 feet under the ocean to find their favorite fish. The oldest recorded bird is an albatross named Wisdom. She is more than 70 years old!

## FIND AND CIRCLE THE NAMES OF THESE SEABIRD SPECIES IN THIS WORD SEARCH.

ALBATROSS

PUFFIN

PELICAN

GULL

LOON

PENGUIN

PETREL

TERN

```
H  H  B  N  S  A  H  N  M  G  U  L  L  I  E
E  Q  W  V  A  L  U  S  T  M  P  T  T  U  F
B  F  T  N  Q  B  B  P  V  B  I  F  L  V  N
H  C  S  I  P  A  G  E  D  E  W  A  Y  H  U
K  Z  J  G  J  T  E  L  E  R  T  E  P  C  O
M  Z  Q  J  U  R  C  I  Z  I  M  X  Z  Y  V
X  R  Z  R  A  O  K  C  Y  Q  M  B  Q  F  Z
U  J  A  Y  Q  S  W  A  F  J  V  O  L  I  J
W  Y  R  W  J  S  J  N  N  C  C  L  U  B  P
X  L  N  Y  P  E  N  G  U  I  N  U  E  U  R
X  C  R  J  G  N  Y  J  D  K  F  O  P  U  I
U  W  E  Q  L  L  A  N  L  O  L  F  X  T  L
X  Y  T  D  Z  O  O  C  V  A  O  T  U  P  I
E  U  R  N  W  B  O  U  Q  V  Q  B  K  P  Q
T  E  T  R  R  H  U  N  T  W  Z  P  U  X  X
```

PUFFINS NEST IN BURROWS ON SEA CLIFFS.
THEIR BABIES ARE CALLED PUFFLINGS. HOW
MANY PUFFINS CAN YOU SPOT IN THIS PICTURE?

# Incredible Invertebrates

It's hard to imagine, but there are a whole lot of animals out there with absolutely no bones. They're called invertebrates—that means "no backbone." Some invertebrates, like shrimp, lobsters, and crabs, have exoskeletons that they shed as they grow. Others, like jellyfish, anemones, squid, and octopuses, stay soft and flexible all their lives. An octopus has a beak like a bird and can squeeze through *any* opening that's bigger than its beak. Not all invertebrates are small; the lion's mane jellyfish can measure up to 120 feet long!

### YOU CAN MAKE 447 WORDS OUT OF THE LETTERS IN INVERTEBRATE, INCLUDING "NET." CAN YOU LIST EIGHT MORE?

1. _____

2. _____

3. _____

4. _____

5. _____

6. _____

7. _____

8. _____

# THERE ARE LOTS OF INVERTEBRATES HIDING IN THIS PICTURE! CAN YOU FIND A SEA STAR, A JELLYFISH, AN OCTOPUS, A LOBSTER, A HORSESHOE CRAB, AND AN ANEMONE?

# Radical Reptiles

How can you tell a sea snake from a land snake? Sea snakes have flat tails! There are thousands of animals that live in the ocean, but only about 100 of them are reptiles, and 60 of those are snakes. There are seven species of sea turtles, and they lay their eggs on beaches around the world. The marine iguana lives near the Galápagos Islands and can hold its breath for 30 minutes! The saltwater crocodile is the biggest reptile on Earth—males can reach 1,200 pounds and 17 feet long.

## MATCH THE CLUES ON THE LEFT SIDE WITH THE CORRECT ANSWERS ON THE RIGHT SIDE.

1. Where marine iguanas live
2. The biggest reptile in the world
3. Number of species of sea turtles
4. The marine iguana can hold its breath this long
5. Number of ocean reptile species
6. Sea snakes have this kind of tail

A. 7

B. 30 minutes

C. flat

D. Galápagos

E. 100

F. saltwater crocodile

# USE THE KEY BELOW TO COLOR THE VENOMOUS YELLOW-BELLIED SEA SNAKE.

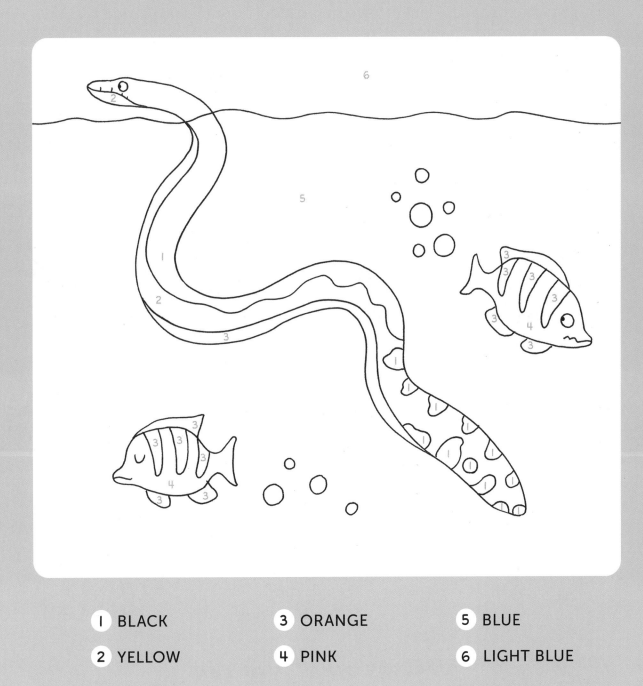

1 BLACK     3 ORANGE     5 BLUE

2 YELLOW     4 PINK     6 LIGHT BLUE

# Marvelous and Microscopic

The ocean is full of amazing things that you can't see without looking through a microscope. Plankton are microscopic organisms carried around by the currents. There are two kinds: phytoplankton (plants) and zooplankton (animals). Phytoplankton are the base of the whole ocean food web. They get energy from the sun and then zooplankton eat them. Then bigger things eat the zooplankton—all the way up to what you eat for dinner! If there were no plankton in the ocean, there would be no other fish, sharks, or whales, because they'd have nothing to eat.

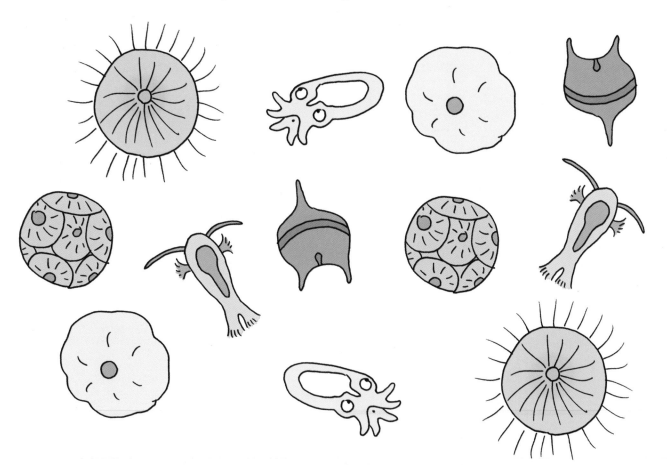

YOU'D BE SURPRISED BY WHAT YOU CAN SEE UNDER A MICROSCOPE! CAN YOU FIND SIX MATCHING MICROORGANISMS?

# UNSCRAMBLE THESE MARVELOUS MICROSCOPIC WORDS.

1. KHTOPLYANNPOT _____

2. ODOF BEW _____

3. RERUCNST _____

4. PCEMOIORCS _____

5. POOZANTOKNL _____

6. GNEERY _____

7. ROSGMAINS _____

# Important Plants

Along with phytoplankton, the base of all life in the ocean, important ocean plants include seagrasses, which look like grass on land but grow on the sandy ocean floor. They can form underwater meadows large enough to be seen from space! "Seaweed" is a word used to describe lots of different types of large red, brown, or green algae. Kelp is a type of brown algae that forms massive undersea forests more than 200 feet high! Seaweed and seagrass are important habitats for young fish and sea turtles.

## FILL IN EACH BLANK WITH A WORD FROM THE WORD BANK.

1. Seaweed and seagrass are important _____ for fish and turtles.

2. You can see meadows of _____ from space.

3. The base of all life in the ocean is _____.

4. Kelp is a type of _____ algae.

5. There are undersea forests made of _____.

6. Seaweed describes red, brown, or green _____.

| | | |
|---|---|---|
| ALGAE | HABITATS | KELP |
| BROWN | SEAGRASS | PHYTOPLANKTON |

# KELP FORESTS ARE IMPORTANT HABITATS FOR OTTERS, SEALS, AND FISH. USE THE NUMBER KEY TO COLOR THE KELP FOREST ECOSYSTEM.

1 GREEN

2 BLUE

3 BROWN

4 YELLOW

5 GRAY

6 RED

# Vital Ocean Zones

The deepest point in the ocean is more than 36,000 feet from the surface, but sunlight really only reaches the first 650 feet. Scientists call that the "sunlit zone," and it's where most of the animals in the ocean live. Below that, animals have to adapt to less light, colder temperatures, and higher pressure. The five ocean zones, from the surface down, are sunlit, twilight, midnight, abyssal, and hadal. The twilight zone is cold and light is scarce. In the midnight, abyssal, and hadal zones there is no light at all!

CAN YOU COMPLETE THIS OCEAN ZONES CROSSWORD PUZZLE?

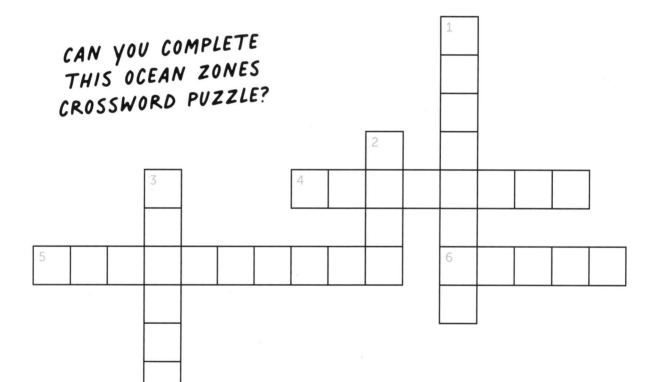

## DOWN

1. This only reaches the first 650 feet of the ocean
2. The number of ocean zones
3. Deeper water is _____ than surface water

## ACROSS

4. Light is scarce in this ocean zone
5. Most of the animals in the ocean live here
6. This zone is in the deepest ocean trenches

FROM THE SURFACE TO THE DEEPEST OCEAN TRENCH, THE OCEAN IS FULL OF LIFE. COLOR THE ANIMALS THAT LIVE IN THE OCEAN.

# Deep-Sea Life

It's easy to think that nothing could live in the darkest, coldest depths of the ocean, but lots of animals evolved to thrive in the pitch black and high pressure. Only about 2 percent of all ocean species spend their lives in the deep ocean zones. Lots of them glow in the dark using special organs in their bodies—it's called bioluminescence. The female anglerfish uses a glowing lure in front of its head to lure prey into its big toothy mouth!

THE DEEP-SEA VAMPIRE SQUID CAN FLIP ITSELF
INSIDE OUT WHEN THREATENED! COLOR THE
SQUID SWIMMING, FLOATING, AND SCARED.

# FIND AND CIRCLE THE NAMES OF THESE DEEP-SEA ANIMALS IN THIS WORD SEARCH.

```
O  T  R  P  K  Z  W  I  C  Q  B  U  P  K  S
H  A  U  I  G  T  G  F  I  G  T  T  A  K  Y
Q  C  D  M  D  V  I  C  W  U  U  B  N  C  I
N  G  I  M  V  E  R  W  K  B  B  V  J  A  D
H  V  N  P  L  F  Y  H  Q  L  E  R  B  W  A
L  A  T  P  Y  R  U  R  D  O  W  N  S  G  O
U  K  R  A  H  S  N  I  L  B  O  G  X  I  A
N  F  C  E  K  H  G  M  W  F  R  P  R  A  P
E  R  U  J  A  O  S  Z  H  I  M  M  U  N  V
I  F  R  M  E  M  V  I  E  S  Z  M  W  T  A
C  N  G  F  O  U  I  B  F  H  K  H  W  S  D
U  Z  P  X  O  D  Q  H  K  G  V  H  R  Q  G
W  R  D  O  P  O  S  I  C  S  A  K  P  U  Z
T  B  N  A  U  T  I  L  U  S  W  H  H  I  O
H  S  H  B  P  S  I  T  R  Z  C  F  F  D  B
```

NAUTILUS     ISOPOD     CHIMAERA

TUBE WORM     GOBLIN SHARK     BLOBFISH

HAGFISH     GIANT SQUID

# The Dynamic Ocean Floor

We know more about the surface of Mars than we do about the bottom of the ocean! We do know there are long underwater mountain ranges and deep trenches, but less than 10 percent of the ocean floor has been mapped by modern technology. The Mariana Trench is the ocean's deepest point. It's seven *miles* below the surface—more than three times the average ocean depth. In 1977, scientists discovered hydrothermal vents: underwater volcanoes where temperatures can reach 700 degrees Fahrenheit! Animals like tube worms, crabs, and octopuses thrive in this harsh environment.

## CRACK THE CODE!

Scientists have a word for animals that live in extreme environments like hydrothermal vents. Can you use the code to find out what it is?

___ ___ ___ ___ ___ ___ ___ ___ ___ ___ ___ ___ ___
9  18  8  4  9  25  6  24  21  1  3  9  11

**KEY**

| 1 | 2 | 3 | 4 | 5 | 6 | 7 | 8 | 9 | 10 | 11 | 12 | 13 |
|---|---|---|---|---|---|---|---|---|----|----|----|----|
| I | D | L | R | J | O | C | T | E | V | S | N | W |

| 14 | 15 | 16 | 17 | 18 | 19 | 20 | 21 | 22 | 23 | 24 | 25 | 26 |
|----|----|----|----|----|----|----|----|----|----|----|----|----|
| K | Y | F | U | X | B | Z | H | Q | A | P | M | G |

WHEN WHALES DIE AND THEIR BODIES SINK
TO THE OCEAN FLOOR, THEY CREATE AMAZING
ECOSYSTEMS FOR DEEP-SEA FISH. CAN YOU SPOT
SIX DIFFERENCES BETWEEN THE TWO WHALE FALLS?

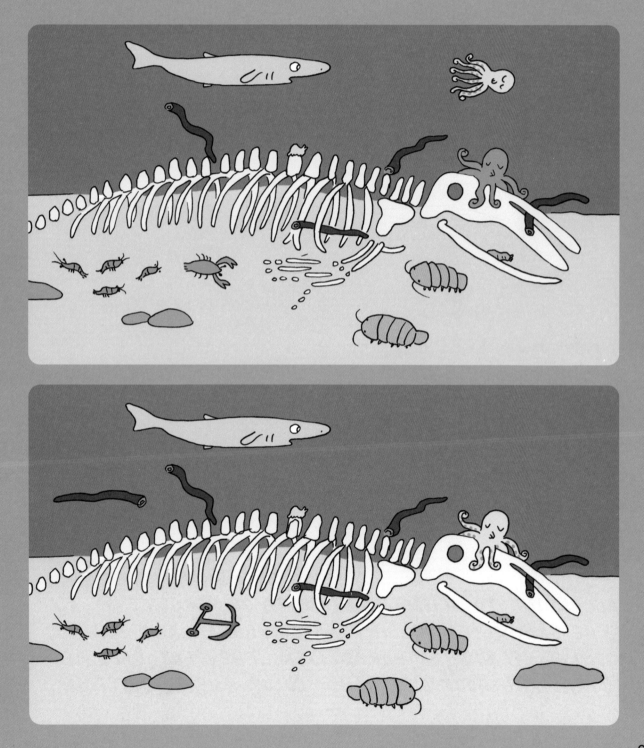

# Critical Coasts

When you think about where the ocean meets the land, you might picture a sandy beach, but that's only one type of coastal environment. Lots of animals and plants live on rocky areas between high and low tide called the rocky intertidal zone. Others live in coastal forests of mangroves, where great big tree roots stick up from the water. Healthy coastal environments are very important, especially where there are structures like houses and roads. They can help stop storms and protect against dangerous flooding.

ACCORDING TO SCIENTISTS, UP TO 70 PERCENT OF ALL THE SANDY BEACHES IN THE CARIBBEAN AND HAWAII EXIST BECAUSE OF PARROTFISH. THEY EAT BITS OF CORAL AND POOP OUT SAND! COLOR THE PARROTFISH.

## CAN YOU UNSCRAMBLE THESE WORDS RELATING TO THE COAST?

1. DASNY ACHEB _____

   _____

2. MROSTS _____

3. CYROK LTIANTEDRI _____

   _____

4. RGVEANOSM _____

5. SEDIT _____

6. TLACAOS _____

# Ocean Motion: Currents

Across the globe, giant currents pull up cold water from the deep ocean and push down warm water from the surface. Scientists call this the "great ocean conveyor belt," and it's important to all life on Earth. The Gulf Stream, which brings warm water from the Gulf of Mexico up the U.S. East Coast and over toward Europe, is an important current. In the Northern Hemisphere, currents go right; in the Southern Hemisphere, they turn left. This "Coriolis effect" occurs because of the way the Earth spins in space.

## TRACE THE NAMES OF SOME OF THE WORLD'S CURRENTS.

HUMBOLDT

GULF STREAM

KUROSHIO

AGULHAS

MONSOON DRIFT

LABRADOR

IN 1992, A SHIP LEAVING HONG KONG LOST 28,000 BATH TOYS OVERBOARD. FOR YEARS, OCEAN CURRENTS MOVED THEM ALL OVER THE WORLD. CONNECT THE DOTS TO SEE THE TOY!

# The Pull of Tides

All along the coasts, the level of the ocean on land changes every day—that's because of tides. The moon's gravity pulls on the Earth's oceans and causes tidal force. That force makes the ocean bulge out on the sides of the Earth closest and farthest from the moon, like squishing a round ball to make an oval. Those bulges are high tide. The Bay of Fundy in Canada has the most dramatic tides in the world—a 38-foot difference between high and low tide!

## FILL IN THE MISSING LETTERS.

1. m __ __ n
2. __ ay o __ F __ __ dy
3. t __ da __ f __ r __ __
4. gr __ v __ ty
5. h __ g __ t __ de
6. l __ w __ id __

ON ROCKY COASTS, ANIMALS ARE
CAUGHT IN POCKETS OF WATER
WHEN THE TIDE GOES OUT.
COLOR THE BUSY TIDE POOL!

# Wave Action

When wind blows over the ocean, it creates ripples that become waves. Those ripples keep moving even after the wind stops. They can travel for days until they "break"—they crash into something like a beach or another wave. The stronger the wind blows, the bigger the waves get. When two storms connect, they can cause "freak waves" (also known as rogue waves) that can be more than 80 feet high. Tsunamis are huge, dangerous waves triggered by large earthquakes. The tallest tsunami ever recorded was in Lituya Bay, Alaska, in 1958—1,700 feet high!

## MATCH THE CLUES ON THE LEFT SIDE WITH THE CORRECT ANSWERS ON THE RIGHT SIDE.

1. This can form when two storms collide

2. These trigger tsunamis

3. This causes waves to form

4. Freak waves can be this high

5. The biggest tsunami happened here

6. What happens when a wave runs into another wave

7. How tall tsunamis can get

A. wind

B. 1,700 feet

C. they break

D. earthquakes

E. freak wave

F. 80 feet

G. Alaska

# THE POLYNESIANS INVENTED SURFING MORE THAN 900 YEARS AGO! HAVE FUN MATCHING THE SURFBOARDS.

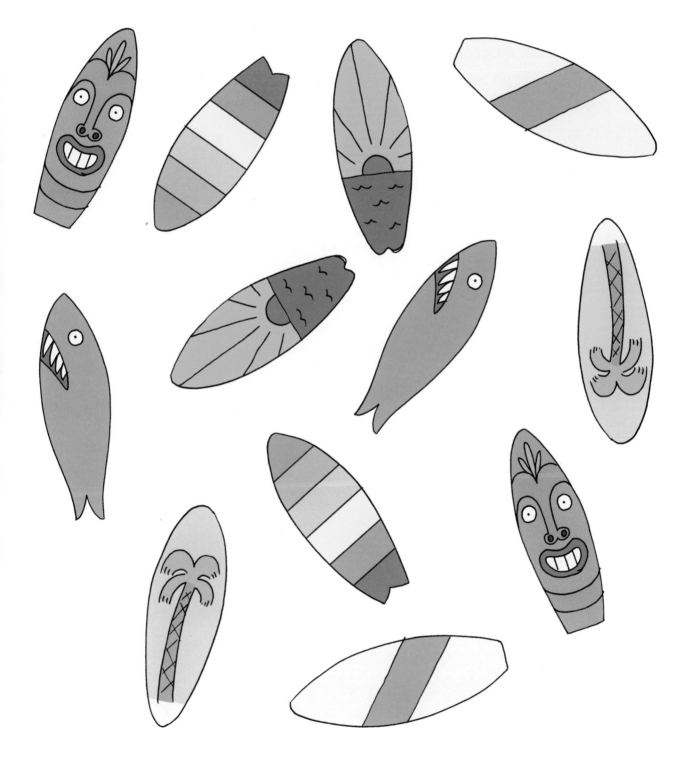

# Wacky Weather

The ocean plays a big part in the weather of the world. It absorbs lots of warmth from the sun, and then currents move that warmth all around the globe. Where the ocean is warmer, more clouds form and more rain falls. Did you know typhoons, hurricanes, and cyclones are all different names for the same type of storm? The only difference is what part of the world they happen in. There are also tornadoes in the ocean, but they're called "waterspouts."

LIGHTHOUSES HELP SHIPS NAVIGATE AT NIGHT AND IN BAD WEATHER. COLOR THE LIGHTHOUSE.

# UNSCRAMBLE THESE WEATHER TERMS.

1. OPYHTNO _____

2. INRA _____

3. RIEHURCNA _____

4. ECLONCY _____

5. REOTSUTAPW _____

6. TRREUNCS _____

7. ADOTRNO _____

# Lively Coral Reefs

Coral reefs are the most diverse areas on planet Earth. They make up only 1 percent of the global ocean but are home to nearly 25 percent of all ocean species—that's millions of kinds of animals! There are so many types of organisms living on coral reefs that scientists sometimes call them the "rainforests of the sea." Corals look like rocks, but they're actually very slow-growing animals. Big barrier reefs (like the Great Barrier Reef near Australia) can take anywhere from 100,000 to 30 million years to fully form.

## FIND AND CIRCLE THE NAMES OF THESE CORAL REEF ANIMALS IN THIS WORD SEARCH.

SEAHORSE

SQUID

OCTOPUS

SPONGE

SEA TURTLE

GIANT CLAM

SEA DRAGON

LOBSTER

```
Q K O S M V M A P X A T E F K
E T R U A A Y M B S J S F K Z
G R W G L G O Q W G R S L G R
Q U T Y C W N X I O E M W R Z
R B D X T U Z Z H W T Q Y I G
R V K C N P S A P S Q U I D B
K P T N A S E A D R A G O N N
N V U M I S A I K U W Z H S Q
M C C B G U T S L O B S T E R
C V M Y H H U O N L A O G Q S
N A U K S M R K Z B M I N H P
L R S U P O T C O V P K I Z O
T F K E I Q L L X Q P Q W Z N
P N B N S K E A P N P U U X G
P X Z I X C R J T U C F V W E
```

CAN YOU HELP THE SCUBA DIVER FIND HER WAY THROUGH THE REEF AND BACK TO HER BOAT?

# Sea Ice, Glaciers, and Icebergs

Glaciers form in cold areas over land where snow falls and is compressed until it turns to ice. Around 10 percent of the world is covered by glaciers, including Greenland and Antarctica. When chunks of glaciers break off into the ocean, icebergs are formed. Sea ice forms when the ocean gets cold enough that the top layer freezes. Warmer temperatures from climate change mean there's less sea ice. That's a big problem for the animals that rely on the ice to survive, like polar bears, arctic foxes, and seals.

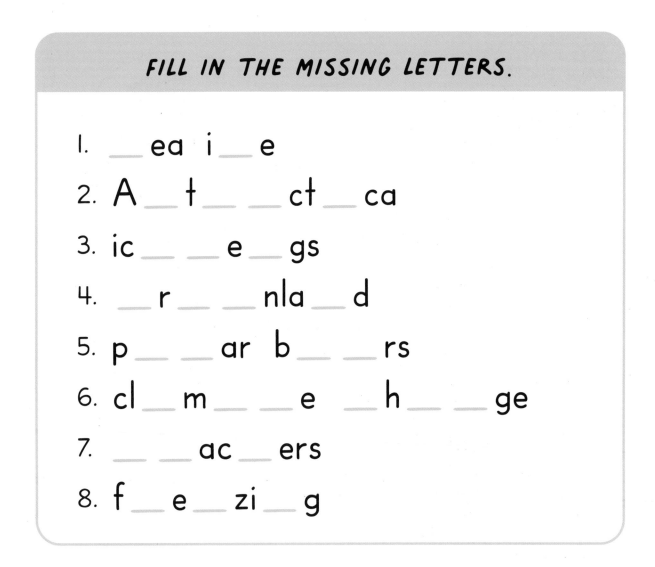

### FILL IN THE MISSING LETTERS.

1. __ ea i__ e
2. A__ t __ __ ct __ ca
3. ic __ __ e __ gs
4. __ r __ __ nla __ d
5. p __ __ ar b __ __ rs
6. cl __ m __ __ e __ h __ __ ge
7. __ __ __ ac __ ers
8. f __ e __ zi __ g

LOTS OF SEALS RELY ON SEA ICE FOR A SAFE
PLACE TO HAVE THEIR BABIES (CALLED PUPS).
CAN YOU MATCH SIX PAIRS OF SEALS?

# Millions of Shipwrecks

For as long as people have been exploring the ocean, their ships have been in danger of sinking from rough seas, bad weather, sea battles, or running aground on coral reefs. There are more than 3 *million* shipwrecks in the world—everything from ancient Greek merchant vessels to World War II submarines to giant container ships carrying goods across the world. With more than 300 shipwrecks in its waters, Bermuda has more wrecks per square mile than anywhere else in the ocean!

SOMETIMES SCIENTISTS SINK OLD SHIPS, SUBWAY CARS, OIL RIGS, OR EVEN TANKS TO CREATE ARTIFICIAL CORAL REEFS. COLOR THE TRAIN CAR REEF.

# CRACK THE CODE!

Use the code to learn the name of one of the world's most famous shipwrecks. When it was built, it was considered "unsinkable"!

$$\overline{\phantom{x}} \quad \overline{\phantom{x}} \quad \overline{\phantom{x}}$$
$$12 \quad 7 \quad 17$$

$$\overline{\phantom{x}} \quad \overline{\phantom{x}} \quad \overline{\phantom{x}} \quad \overline{\phantom{x}} \quad \overline{\phantom{x}} \quad \overline{\phantom{x}} \quad \overline{\phantom{x}}$$
$$6 \quad 3 \quad 6 \quad 24 \quad 25 \quad 3 \quad 8$$

**KEY**

| 1 | 2 | 3 | 4 | 5 | 6 | 7 | 8 | 9 | 10 | 11 | 12 | 13 |
|---|---|---|---|---|---|---|---|---|----|----|----|----|
| D | K | I | F | X | T | M | C | V | Y | L | R | P |

| 14 | 15 | 16 | 17 | 18 | 19 | 20 | 21 | 22 | 23 | 24 | 25 | 26 |
|----|----|----|----|----|----|----|----|----|----|----|----|----|
| B | E | Z | S | O | H | W | Q | J | U | A | N | G |

# Brave Explorers

In the 1520s, Ferdinand Magellan became the first person to sail around the world. But he was far from the first ocean explorer. There's evidence that hundreds of thousands of years ago, early humans crossed the open sea and colonized islands in the Philippines. Exploration is a lot different now! We know almost everything about the surface of the ocean, but the deep is still largely a mystery. Scientists use technology like submarines and drones to explore beneath the surface.

**THROUGHOUT HISTORY, THERE HAVE BEEN LOTS OF WAYS TO EXPLORE UNDER THE SEA. FIND AND CIRCLE THE NAMES OF THESE INVENTIONS IN THIS WORD SEARCH.**

SCUBA

DIVING BELL

BATHYSPHERE

SUBMARINE

ROV

EXOSUIT

SONAR

REBREATHER

```
Y  H  B  D  U  H  M  G  F  Z  C  W  Z  O  I
S  O  N  A  R  M  D  F  D  A  T  R  Z  Y  K
M  F  X  D  P  L  H  F  I  E  O  H  V  Z  S
D  N  Q  P  K  B  H  Y  V  V  N  Q  I  W  U
F  Y  O  C  F  S  F  A  I  G  N  S  C  Z  B
C  M  V  Y  C  X  C  Y  N  A  N  Y  O  K  M
X  N  U  U  R  R  Q  Z  G  L  E  G  P  F  A
B  G  B  M  F  F  O  U  B  Y  P  B  K  L  R
B  A  T  H  Y  S  P  H  E  R  E  J  C  H  I
T  Y  I  T  W  L  J  Z  L  R  U  W  T  Y  N
U  M  E  K  R  B  G  W  L  Z  R  F  W  N  E
K  I  I  F  V  C  O  R  B  P  Z  G  V  V  U
R  E  B  R  E  A  T  H  E  R  Y  L  J  B  Y
I  L  Q  S  P  E  X  O  S  U  I  T  R  L  C
R  R  P  P  S  X  Z  L  D  C  X  Y  I  W  S
```

IN 1898, JOSHUA SLOCUM BECAME THE FIRST
PERSON TO SAIL ALONE AROUND THE WORLD.
THE JOURNEY TOOK MORE THAN THREE YEARS!
CONNECT THE DOTS TO SEE HIS SHIP.

# Climate Change and You

Earth's climate is getting warmer because of pollution, deforestation, and other human activities. Hotter temperatures mean more unpredictable weather and bigger storms. The ocean is so big that it absorbs a lot of this excess heat, and those rising temperatures affect the animals that live in the ocean. Scientists and governments around the world are working together to help slow the effects of climate change. By making smart choices like taking the bus, buying reusable items, and eating less meat, you can do your part. Together, we can make a difference!

## ARE THESE CLIMATE FACTS TRUE OR FALSE?

1. Human activities are causing climate change.
   TRUE FALSE

2. The ocean absorbs excess heat. TRUE FALSE

3. Ocean animals aren't affected by climate change.
   TRUE FALSE

4. Warmer temperatures impact the weather. TRUE FALSE

5. There's no way to slow climate change. TRUE FALSE

6. Climate change means Earth's temperature is getting warmer. TRUE FALSE

HUMAN ACTIVITIES ARE CAUSING CLIMATE CHANGE. PEOPLE WHO MAKE BETTER CHOICES CAN HELP THE ENVIRONMENT. CAN YOU SPOT SIX DIFFERENCES BETWEEN THESE TWO PICTURES?

# Answer Key

## Page 15

biodiversity

## Page 16

## Page 17

1. BIGGEST
2. MARIANA
3. VOLCANOES
4. ISLANDS
5. SUBMERSIBLE
6. FISH

## Page 19

Greenland shark

## Page 21

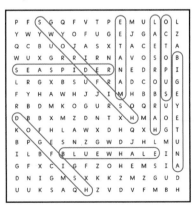

## Page 24

## Page 25

1. warmest
2. landlocked
3. coral reefs
4. currents
5. India
6. third

## Page 26

1. Antarctica
2. emperor penguin
3. elephant seal
4. orca whale
5. Southern Ocean

## Page 33

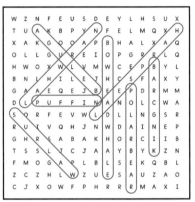

## Page 37

## Page 38

1. coral reefs
2. Pacific Ocean
3. Australia
4. astronauts
5. islands

## Page 41

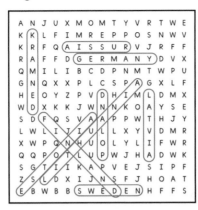

## Page 43

1. NORTH
2. WHALES
3. PACIFIC
4. ANIMALS
5. SAKHALIN
6. TIDES

## Page 44

Hokkaido

## Page 45

13 birds

## Page 49

1. sediment
2. people
3. China
4. rivers
5. color
6. scientists

## Page 50

## Page 53

1. False
2. True
3. True
4. False
5. False

## Page 55

Cayman Trough

## Page 57

## Page 58

1. *Sargassum*
2. North Atlantic Gyre
3. Bermuda
4. garbage patch
5. seaweed
6. currents

## Page 60

1. Indian Ocean
2. tectonic
3. Thailand
4. Andaman Islands
5. trade route
6. earthquakes

## Page 62

Zalzala Koh

## Page 65

## Page 67

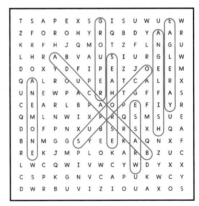

## Page 68

1. 1841
2. invertebrates
3. Ross Ice Shelf
4. southernmost
5. James Clark Ross
6. 100

## Page 70

1. F
2. C
3. A
4. D
5. B
6. E

## Page 71

## Page 72

## Page 74

1. Nunavut
2. belugas
3. Arctic Ocean
4. walruses
5. polar bears
6. Quebec

## Page 75

## Page 78

chungungo, also known as "sea cat"

## Page 81

1. BONES
2. CARTILAGE
3. GREENLAND
4. WHALE
5. FISH
6. *MOLA MOLA*

## Page 82

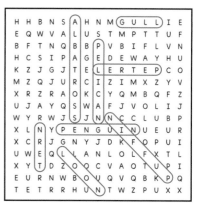

## Page 83

11 puffins

## Page 85

## Page 86

1. D
2. F
3. A
4. B
5. E
6. C

**Page 89**

1. phytoplankton
2. food web
3. currents
4. microscope
5. zooplankton
6. energy
7. organisms

**Page 90**

1. habitats
2. seagrass
3. phytoplankton
4. brown
5. kelp
6. algae

**Page 92**

1. SUNLIGHT
2. FIVE
3. COLDER
4. TWILIGHT
5. SUNLIT ZONE
6. HADAL

**Page 95**

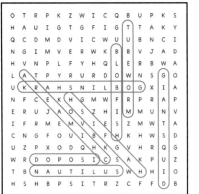

**Page 96**

extremophiles

**Page 97**

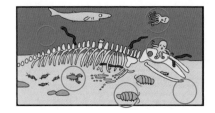

**Page 99**

1. sandy beach
2. storms
3. rocky intertidal
4. mangroves
5. tides
6. coastal

**Page 102**

1. moon
2. Bay of Fundy
3. tidal force
4. gravity
5. high tide
6. low tide

**Page 104**

1. E
2. D
3. A
4. F
5. G
6. C
7. B

**Page 107**

1. typhoon
2. rain
3. hurricane
4. cyclone
5. waterspout
6. currents
7. tornado

**Page 108**

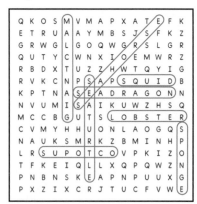

**Page 109**

## Page 110

1. sea ice
2. Antarctica
3. icebergs
4. Greenland
5. polar bears
6. climate change
7. glaciers
8. freezing

## Page 113

RMS *Titanic*

## Page 114

```
Y H B D U H M G F Z C W Z O I
S O N A R M D F D A T R Z Y K
M F X D P L H F I E O H V Z S
D N Q P K B H Y V V N Q I W U
F Y O C F S F A I G N S C Z B
C M V Y C X C Y N A N Y O K M
X N U U R R Q Z G L E G P F A
B G B M F F O U B Y P B K L R
B A T H Y S P H E R E J C H I
T Y I T W L J Z L R U W T Y N
U M E K R B G W L Z R F W N E
K I I F V C O R B P Z G V V U
R E B R E A T H E R Y L J B Y
I L Q S P E X O S U I T R L C
R R P P S X Z L D C X Y I W S
```

## Page 117

## Page 116

1. True
2. True
3. False
4. True
5. False
6. True

# About the Author

**EMILY GREENHALGH** is an award-winning science journalist whose work has been featured in *USA Today*, *The Boston Globe*, Gizmodo, the World Meteorological Organization, and in science textbooks. She grew up in Rhode Island, staring into tide pools and dreaming about becoming a mermaid. Realizing that wasn't an actual job, she trained to become a marine biologist and then a science journalist. Now Emily helps scientists tell their stories. She loves discovering what makes research exciting and turning complex science into easy-to-understand ideas. She has worked on commercial fishing boats, tagged breeding sharks, and hiked in Antarctica. In her spare time, she writes speculative fiction and enjoys putting cheese on things. She lives on Cape Cod, Massachusetts, with her husband, their two dogs, and one semi-tolerant cat. Visit emilygreenhalgh.com for more information.

# About the Artist

**CANDELA FERRÁNDEZ** is a freelance illustrator based in Barcelona, Spain. After studying fine arts at Salamanca University, she earned a postgraduate degree in illustration at EINA (Barcelona). When she was a child, she loved looking for bugs and little animals around gardens. Now she draws them. Children, flowers, plants, and animals define her personal universe, which she also expresses in ceramic pieces. Her illustrations have been published by, among others, Milan Presse, Éditions Larousse, Fleurus, and Penguin Random House, including those in *Fun with 50 States* and *Fun with National Parks*. Visit Candela online at candelaferrandez.com.

# Explore your world with 100 or more fun activities and cool facts in every BIG book!

Learn more about the amazing United States, take a virtual trip that reveals hidden attractions, and have fun with activities and wacky facts.

Explore spectacular vistas and delightful surprises in all 63 national parks, including fascinating facts about their landscape, geological features, animals, history, and more.

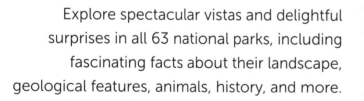

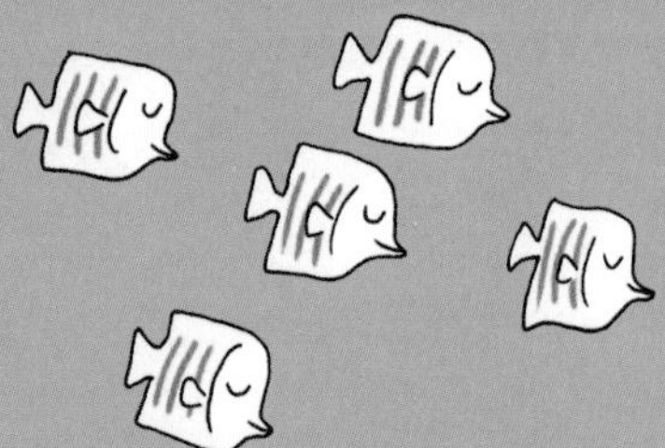